I0492696

Ray Moore UK

Copyright © by Ray Moore

First Edition 2018

Design and Illustrations
Bob Whitebeard Luck
www.whitebeardarts.co.uk

For every
business owner
pursuing their dream
and their families
for supporting them

GEORGE'S PURSUIT ACROSS THE PERILOUS OCEAN

THE TALE OF A BUSINESS ADVENTURE FROM START UP TO FINANCIAL FREEDOM

RAY MOORE

Nautical George and his Five Hats

Part 1 - Introduction

One born every minute

The UK is bursting with entrepreneurial spirit.

The numbers say it all.

In 2016, registrations of new businesses with Companies House hit a record high at just over 600,000. That's a new business springing to life at an incredible rate of more than one every minute!

The trends suggest this is no flash in the pan. Year on year, the numbers of new businesses emerging into the UK economy have been increasing at an accelerated rate. Going into business has truly become part of the British culture.

But, isn't there another statistic out there?

On average a staggering 45% of those business start-ups will fail within 5 years. (UK Government Statistics 2016).

It leaves you wondering just how some people do it. How does anyone turn their fledgling 'money-maker' into a bigger, more successful and profitable business?

This question of what enables one business to grow when another fails (or stagnates) is something which my other two books cover in greater detail.

Both books describe the five distinct Levels of growth that a business reaches on its journey from a start-up to an organisation at the top end of what is classified as a 'medium' sized enterprise.

From fifteen years of working with business owners at all of these Levels, I've found that understanding what is going on and what the owner has to do to move up a Level can become complex.

In my other book, I used a metaphor which

described the Levels of growth in business in terms of different boat types. Interestingly, when asked, most readers could easily associate their business with one of these boats.

I'm well aware that the business world is full of metaphors and buzz words (and these can get a little tiring). Time is money, careers are ladders, strategy is a game of chess and ideas come in boxes... or outside of them, of course!

My aim with the boat metaphor is not to stir up the already muddy waters, but rather to clarify them.

By identifying what defines a Day Tripping boat (representing the new business start-up) and following this through all the way to a Fleet of Cruise Liners, we can create a picture of how businesses behave at different Levels - how many people they employ, what those people do, how they fare among the competition and what pitfalls they face.

By identifying the owner of these businesses in their various Skipper/ Captain's attire, we also get a picture of how they behave - what they do, how they spend their time, what they are aiming for, what internal conflicts they have to deal with and so on.

Before we go any further, let me give you the 5-minute version of what each boat and Level looks like.

The Day Tripper (Level 0)

This is where you find those countless fledgling start- ups who, in many cases, would be better classified as self employed individuals. They're moored by the dockside from early sunlight, ready for the scramble amongst all the other Day Trippers for whatever business comes their way.

The boat is run by a Skipper who literally has to do and manage everything, but the boat only has to make him an income to stay afloat. Every day starts with the 'to do' list and ends with the cash count.

The biggest problem faced by most Day Trippers is capacity. They have a limited number of seats and, if one day they're all full, customers will quickly move on to the next available boat. Because of this, they suffer from an ongoing cycle of feast/famine - a situation that is very hard to break.

The Power Boat (Level 1)

Employing around 5-10 people, micro businesses behave like a Power Boat. They're fast and flexible, have low overheads and are quick to react to opportunities around them. This gives them the advantage of often being quicker to the daily action than some other larger boats.

However, tearing through the big wide ocean at such speed can take its toll.

The ocean can get choppy and, even with some good crew mates on board, the owner feels unable to take their hands off the controls for an instant.

The daily race for business takes priority, leaving

barely any time to maintain the boat or develop the team. It's exhausting!

The Fishing Trawler (Level 2)

The Fishing Trawler (a small business) is pretty robust. Its hull is strong enough to withstand some stormy conditions and there's a crew of anything between 10 – 50 people on board (although it's more usually around 15).

While the crew help to haul in and sort the fish, it's the Skipper who knows what kind of fish they're looking for, where to find them and what waters can be safely navigated.

In other words, the business is highly dependent on the owner's knowledge, experience and long, hard working hours. They ensure the boat provides for everyone.

The Fishing Trawler owner may have a good income and standard of living, but they are time-poor.

The business has little value and because they

can't quite bring themselves to trust other crew members yet, it's extremely hard for them to let go of the controls in a way that would take them to the next Level.

The Cruise Liner (Level 3)

The gleaming Cruise Liner has a Captain at the helm and a crew of between 50 and 100 people. It's the equivalent of a medium sized business and is at a Level where it is large enough to weather most storms.

The Captain might spend some of their time on the Bridge but might equally leave it to be run by other senior crew while they build relationships with passengers or other members of the team.

With the right supporting crew members and systems in place, the owner of this type of boat/ business has a choice. They can remain as Captain if they wish or install a new Captain while spending more of their time on shore, knowing the ship is in safe hands.

The Fleet (Level 4)

Businesses which make it to the top end of the 'medium sized' classification can be compared to a Fleet of Cruise Liners.

Employing between 100 – 250 people, they are often on the brink of becoming something even bigger.

To get to this Level, the owner has simply multiplied everything that took the business to the Cruise Liner stage so that one Cruise Liner became two, then three and so on.

Collectively the Fleet now has enough momentum to weather stormy seas without missing a beat.

The owner can make an appearance on one of the ships now and then but is far more likely to take a back seat, perhaps sitting on the tropical island as the Fleet sail by.

Jumping ship

Perhaps you already have an idea of which type of boat you are running and at which Level that places your business.

If you do, I'd like you to keep an open mind about it for the moment as, by the time you finish reading this book, you may find you're in a completely different part of the ocean.

The big question, however, is what you do if you want to move things up a Level.

You can't just strap on a life jacket, jump overboard and swim up to the new ship to take your place as Captain! Growing a business through the Levels just doesn't happen that way.

Each stage of development requires a process which I've termed Transition – a period when changes must be made both to the business and within the owner's mindset.

For many reasons, the most difficult Transition comes when a Level 2 small business (the Fishing Trawler) attempts to become a Level 3 medium business (the Cruise Liner).

I hope this will become clearer for you as you read the rest of this book and witness the evolution of a business up the Levels as illustrated through the story of one business owner, George.

We'll first meet George when he's an eager twenty-something with an early stage business start-up and then follow him throughout his life until the moment he eventually watches his Fleet pass by from a tropical island.

As his company grows, we'll catch a glimpse of how George feels about the business (his mindset) and watch him as he approaches some of the difficult Transition issues which can stall or prohibit growth. Throughout, I'll be offering a short commentary with some guidance as to what George might do to overcome those difficulties.

While you read George's story, there are four things I'd like you to bear in mind about Transition, all of which are essential components of taking a business to a higher Level.

1. Having a vision

No-one can grow their business successfully without a vision about where they want that business to go.

The end-goal has to be clear so that every business decision can be aligned to it.

2. Keeping the business in balance

There are four key drivers of any business (money, delivery, team, and time) which must be kept in balance to survive Transition. In the early stages of a business, everything is probably about money (cash in and out) and delivery (doing the job). Progressing up the Levels requires much more: good financial structures and information; delivery that is focused on customer experience; and a knowledgeable and skilled team.

Crucially, the way the owner uses their time also needs re-balancing. (See Mindset below.)

3. Setting out the stall

To 'set out the stall' for growth, the business owner needs to review what has been done so far, take time to understand it and then make changes that will support the future business they are aiming for.

It's all about reinforcing the foundations before you approach the Transition.

Think of it like this: you cannot build a Cruise Liner on the same hull as the Power Boat!

4. Mindset

In my second book on the Levels, I compared the changing mindset of business owners at different Levels to an owner wearing a series of different hats.

This starts with a 'Worker' hat where the owner's focus is purely on the daily 'doing' and moves up to an 'Owner' hat where someone may take a back seat but is still involved in identifying priorities for the business and guiding the team of leaders they've installed below them.

In the middle are 'Supervisor' and 'Manager' hats which roughly equate to the Fishing Trawler/ Level 2 small business and the Cruise Liner/ Level 3 medium business.

As I said before, the Transition between these two stages of business development is one of the hardest any business owner must make.

The main reason is the huge mindset difference between the 'Supervisor' and 'Manager' hats – one involving the owner spending time in their business and the other requiring them to work on their business. Making that kind of mindset leap can be extremely challenging.

As George's business grows, we'll see how he tackles (and sometimes struggles) with these key areas - his vision, the drivers of his business, how to set out his stall for growth and how to change his mindset (particularly how he manages that leap from Level 2 to 3).

As you watch him wearing his different hats,

please take a moment to think about the role he is playing in his business – and how this applies to you!

George is his own boss!

Part 2 – Meet George

At twenty-something, George had been working in sales for some time, flitting around the corporate world with a vague notion that there was something better 'out there'.

Unhappy with the way things were going at his last place of work and with a bright idea in mind, George decided to bite the bullet and go it alone.

So here he is, the proud owner of a Day Tripping boat, doing business day-by-day on his own terms.

It's early morning and, like every day, George pulls on his 'beanie' hat as he runs out to get a head start on the 'to do' list - picking up supplies on the way to work, getting the boat ready and putting out the A-board to promote today's trips.

He grabs a coffee and takes a moment to chat with some of the other Boat owners along the dock before the first tourists emerge for the day. (Do the terms 'breakfast' and 'networking' ring any bells?)

George is completely hands-on with his business, doing everything from sales and marketing to washing down the decks.

He often feels like there are not enough hours in the day to get everything done but there's only himself to worry about so, if he makes enough money to live comfortably, George is content. He 'can't afford' to hire some help and, even if he could, how would he find someone who he could trust?

Having been in business about a year, George finds that some days there's more of a scramble for passing trade than others.

One day, the boat is packed and there's no time for that breakfast club; the next he's knocking down prices on the A-board in the afternoon in the hope that he'll get the boat out at least once that day.

It's 'feast' or 'famine'!

Right now, George is enjoying a 'feast' period. Today, he gets particularly lucky as a large group of English language students pass by.

Doing his best imitation of a market stall holder, he calls out the details of his day trips and catches their attention. Tickets sold and off they go.

All George has to do is steer the right way and

wow them with his knowledge of the coastline.

Later on (like he does every day), George counts up the spoils and gives the boat a quick maintenance check before heading home.

To give us an idea of how he feels about his business, let's take a look at some of George's social media updates over the past year:

> **Status:** George is officially in business. No more answering to someone else. From now on, I'm doing it all my way – just call me Boss!

> **Status:** Can't believe I waited so long to start my own business. Yeah, it's a dawn to dusk job but hey, that's what coffee is for, right?

> **Status:** Picked up a bunch of students today and took them around the bay all day – Sun, Sea and... well, it's still early ;)

Status: Life is sweeeeet!

Wow, everything is going so well. George survived the slow start of his fledgling business and now things have really picked up.

It turns out those English language students were from a nearby University which has recently increased its student body.

The good news for George is that they went straight back and told everyone how good the day trip was.

As a result, George is now taking the boat out at least three times a day and every seat is taken.

Some days he even has to turn people away because there just aren't enough seats available.

"I'd let you on standing if I could" he tries to explain, "But, you know, there's health and safety to think about. Come back tomorrow though. I'm sure I'll be able to fit you in."

The problem is George's disappointed

customers are not really interested in coming back another day. They've just spotted another Day Tripper along the dock - a newer, shinier boat with a Skipper that's currently knocking down his prices...

George notices his clients are dwindling.

At first, he assumes it's a temporary glitch (perhaps the students have gone home for mid-term break).

Anyway, he's sure they'll be back soon and meanwhile, he's earned enough to keep afloat, so why not take a moment to relax.

A few weeks later, George is still waiting for some passing trade to pitch up.

He's getting fed up of languishing on the boat, cash flow is dwindling, and he is starting to feel a bit sun burnt.

As his business enters the 'famine' period, George's social media updates start to change:

Status: Anyone up for a day trip around the coast today? Great mates rates available!

Status: Up all night working on some new trip schedules.... But who needs sleep!

Status: Heading out to Shark Bay today. Water might be a bit choppy, but we're guaranteed an adventure. Tickets still available. (Please share).

Status: Just spent the whole morning networking at the Boat Club. That's a few hours of my life I'll never get back but hopefully it might bring in a bit of business.

Status: Someone just asked me if they could book a tour next month! I don't know what I'm doing tomorrow, yet alone next month!

Commentary

Like most owners of business start-ups, George is a one-man army. His beanie hat comes with the 'Worker' mindset - focused entirely on the daily 'doing' and hard graft.

He's doing everything in the business and, with no other crew members on board, the business can only cope with a certain level of custom.

His Day Tripper reacts to passing trade but, every time it gets too popular, George will face the same issues of having to turn people away.

He could be stuck in the feast/ famine cycle indefinitely. George puts time into the business (long hard hours) but it's a straightforward money exchange with no thought to future planning.

Without a consistent business, George is not prepared to employ anyone. It's such a big commitment to get enough work to feed another mouth.

So, what should George do?

Ok, the first thing to say is it depends on what he actually wants for his business. If he's happy having this kind of 'lifestyle' business then that's fine but let's assume he actually does have a vision and wants to take his business up a Level.

George's failing is in fact a very common one. Word of mouth recommendations can often launch a start- up business into a period of growth. George's capacity problems stem from the fact that, like many in his situation, he was unprepared for the challenge. He has not set out the stall to allow for growth.

What he really needs to do is review the foundations of his business and then resource it so that, the next time he attempts to move it up a Level, capacity is no longer the thing that knocks it down.

George might start by researching the nearby University and overseas student market more, so he can drive the business in a way that better meets their needs.

He could take his cue from the person who asked him for a tour next month and set up a new advance booking system that leaves no room for client disappointment.

To prepare for increased demand, he might consider raising some additional finance, perhaps in the form of share capital or a bank loan that would enable him to upgrade the boat or take on those additional crew members.

The point is George has lots of options. He doesn't have to be stuck forever with a beanie hat which, at times, is pulled down so far that it's limiting his view. If he wants to trade it in for something else, George must roll up the edges of that hat and take a good look around him.

Now is the time to change his focus from the passing trade at the dockside and start looking a little further out to sea.

"Learn a new habit"

c

No-one beats George to the action!

A few years later, George heads out the door early in the morning, pulling on his baseball cap back-to-front as he goes.

He's ready for a long day's business and has no expectations of getting home again until late that evening.

George took some advice and managed to take his business up a Level by investing in an upgrade to the boat and bringing in a small crew.

There's now a handful of support staff that help George with some key areas (especially anything that keeps the money rolling in).

As a result of everything he's done so far, George's Day Tripper has evolved into something smarter, faster and more flexible - the Power Boat.

Gone are the days when 'Beanie George' scrabbled for passing trade at the docks. Chasing sales is now the number one priority.

There are opportunities everywhere out at sea and the Power Boat is quick to react, hurtling through the water to beat the others to the action.

It's the middle of February and here's George making a list of everything that needs doing before the end of the current tax year.

There's that engine fault to look at, the staff rotas to organise, a mountain of invoices to enter on 'the system', the current job to finish, late payments to chase and (of course) that new sale to be won.

Frustrated with how much there is to be done, George barks out the orders at the nearest member of staff but barely gives them time to get started on their 'to do' lists before he jumps in and takes over (because it will just be quicker that way).

As Skipper of the Power Boat, George is driven entirely by the business prospects he sees around him and the need to take the advantage before someone else does.

He's working all hours and hasn't had a holiday in two years... but he loves the hustle and bustle... he couldn't be happier!

George receives an invitation to his High School Reunion and, although it will mean an evening away from the boat, he accepts. It will be great to see some old friends (and maybe show off just a little bit).

Let's listen in to a conversation George is having with his friend, Paul.

Paul: Hey George. Good to see you mate. It's been, what, 3 years?

George: Yeah, you know me... busy, busy!

Paul: Of course. How's it all going? You still running that boat?

George: What, the Day Tripper? No way. Got the latest Power Boat now and well, I don't want to boast, but we're pretty much top of our game. The other day we had literally just clinched a deal with one client when we spotted another being chatted up by one of our rivals. Do you know what we did?

Paul: No idea mate.

George: Sped up to them and pulled the contract right from under their noses. Another sale in the bag!

Paul: Sounds good.

George: It's more than good. I've got a crew on board now. They're mostly useless of course. Couldn't steer the boat between them! So I'm still doing just about everything while paying these guys to do... well, I'm not sure what they're doing all day. But, it's great to be the boss!

Paul: So, not much free time then? Guess that's why you couldn't make it to my wedding last year?

George: Yeah, sorry about that. We were right in the middle of a big deal and I had to be on deck 24/7. How did it go?

Paul: Best day of my life! Couldn't have been better.

George: Great, great... so what are you up to these days anyway?

Paul: Still in IT, working for a consultancy firm in Exeter...

George: Slave to the wage, eh? Don't know why you don't get out of that rat race and start your own business. Once you've done it, you'll never want to work for anyone else again. Oh, talking of business, our on-board computer keeps crashing. Do you reckon you could come take a look some time?

George and Paul agree to catch up again in a few weeks.

Meanwhile, a new potential client has shown up in the water and George and his crew are heading out to reel them in.

There are about ten other Power Boats nearby but the sales pitch is prepared and George couldn't be more confident about winning this race.

They're half way there when the weather changes, the ocean gets choppy and suddenly the client seems to be moving further away. George had been unaware that any stormy weather was coming and immediately rounds on a member of the crew for not telling him or doing something about it.

However, everyone had been so focused on the sales pitch that there had been no time to check the forecast.

The boat's maintenance has also fallen by the wayside and, without any training or experience in navigating such choppy waters, the crew are rapidly turning a shade of green.

With the waves rising above them, George knows he should slow down, look at the forecast, make sure the boat is secure, check how the team are doing and maybe even plan a new route.

But, he cannot let go of that steering wheel even for a moment and besides, the chase to that sale is still on.

Thanks to George's skill and expertise, eventually the Power Boat arrives at the client's base and somehow, he manages to win the pitch. However, the boat is now in dire need of repair and the crew have taken a pounding.

Exhausted, two members decide they've had enough and give their resignation.

With no time to stop (even for a moment to celebrate the win), George reaches for his old beanie hat and gets stuck into fixing the boat.

Under his comfortable beanie, he can be seen working through the night, muttering under his breath about the two deserters:

"Suppose they just didn't have what it takes. No point trying to replace them though. I always did everything before... wasn't it better that way?"

So, George keeps at the daily tasks formerly carried out by his crew members while still trying to race the boat (and what's left of his crew) to the next sale.

George still loves the excitement this brings but, after a while, even he can see that the boat is barely winning any new business (although everyone is still getting a good soaking)!

With depleted resources and energy, the Power Boat is soon in the even more unhappy position where fulfilling existing contracts on time becomes impossible.

George may be a smooth talker but constantly having to make excuses to clients about delays is becoming irritating. He frequently retreats to working on the engine instead – it's noisy there so he can easily ignore his clients' messages.

At sunset, as he's drying off once again, George looks up and spots a Fishing Trawler coming into the harbour. The crew are in full waterproofs and yellow sou'westers and for a moment, George pictures himself as the happy Skipper of such a vessel. Before he can imagine the scene any further, his phone beeps with a new text message.

Paul: Everyone's in the Axe & Compass tonight. You still coming?

George: Sorry mate, got caught up. Another time!

Commentary

George is running a micro-business which can react quickly to opportunities but only if George holds tight to the controls at all times. Let go for a moment and the Power Boat will sink!

With his baseball cap on, George is stuck in a

'Supervisor' mindset.

He may be thinking in terms of the weekly or monthly (rather than a daily) schedule but it's still short-term.

Now, when he goes over the 'to do' lists, he allocates tasks to his staff (not goals) and then too often jumps in because he thinks he'll be able to do them quicker and better.

George is chasing and taking every available order. While the bank balance is good enough to fund his lifestyle (for now), other essential drivers of his business are rapidly going out of balance.

Very typically for a business at this Level, delivery can't keep up with sales.

As for his team, George not only fails to develop them by passing on his understanding and knowledge but he also barely understands what they're doing – meaning he's not setting them any kind of priorities.

So, what should he do?

The way I see it, there are three areas George needs to address:

1. **Learn a new habit**

   George is so close to the coalface that he has no idea of what's coming up next and only reacts to changing conditions as they descend on him.

   To avoid repeatedly getting into this position, George should be making a new habit of checking the forecast.

   By regularly seeking up-to-date information (on markets/ trends etc.) George will be able to see what changes lie ahead much clearer and be better equipped to respond to them with the right business decisions.

2. **Get things back in balance**

   There is really no point in George winning every sale if he cannot follow-through on delivery. If he carries on this way, eventually customer dissatisfaction will lead to loss of sales and loss of money.

So, George should stop, reflect and review how his business is operating now and how he is spending his time, then make a change.

If he's currently spending 90% of his time on sales, then some of that must be re-allocated to other areas – maintaining the boat, developing the team and identifying what customers want (and expect) from delivery.

3. Get out of his comfort zone

It is obvious that George would much rather continue chasing new orders than spend time setting priorities (for himself, his boat and his team) or take a long hard look at his declining record of customer service. In this way, George is very comfortable with his baseball cap mindset.

However, there are times when George retreats

into a former comfort zone, pulling on the beanie so he can get stuck into the job at hand. This is comfortable for George because he knows he can do what's needed of him in that role – fixing the boat in the early hours and so on!

If George really wants to take his business up a Level, the focus of the whole Power Boat needs to shift from winning a single race to winning the tournament.

George's back-to-front baseball cap needs some straightening out (and perhaps he even needs to find something more waterproof) so he can refocus on the long-term priorities. It's a change in mindset that won't always feel comfortable but that is no excuse to avoid it!

"Get things back in balance"

Gone fishing

After a period at the top of the league in his Power Boat business, George realised that what got him there wasn't going to take him or his business any further.

Working harder and longer hours just wasn't going to cut it.

Finally understanding that he would have to start relying on others a bit more, George is now the proud Skipper of a Fishing Trawler with a 15-strong crew to help maintain the boat, haul in the nets, sort, store and sell the catch.

The sea throws all kinds of troublesome conditions at the trawler but, while increased overheads make it slower, it is also strong and sturdy enough to face the ocean swell.

The Fishing Trawler regularly brings in a good catch. A good proportion of this has to be pumped back into the boat and there are times when it has to trudge back to dock for lengthy, expensive repairs.

However, George knows where to find his fish and overall there's enough to go around. Married to Kay with two young children, George is proud of his role as provider – for his family and for everyone working on the boat.

He still must leave the house early and gets home late but George and his family enjoy a good income and they've had some great holidays (even if the tablet comes with them).

So, here's the Trawler out at sea with the crew busy hauling in the nets.

Meanwhile George (nice and dry under his yellow sou'wester hat) has spent the early morning interpreting the forthcoming weather conditions, looking at his quarterly targets and managing customer relations.

Looking up, George spots a fairly new member of the crew, Liam, sorting the fish and getting it all wrong.

He runs out on deck to set things straight. Here's an abridged version of their conversation:

George: Liam, what on Earth are you doing?

Liam: Sorting the catch, boss.

George: But that's not how you do it. We only want these fish (points to a turbot) and not these ones (points to a plaice). So, one goes in the tub, the other gets thrown back to sea – got it?

Liam: Err, yeah, OK. But why don't we want these other ones too?

George: Why? It doesn't matter why, just get on with it. I haven't spent the last 6 months increasing turbot orders by 30% and the last month bringing us to where we can find the best turbot only for you to spend all day bagging plaice! What am I supposed to do with that?

Liam: Sorry boss, I'm just not sure how to spot the difference.

George: Right, you go and wash down the
               deck and I'll take over here!

Up on deck, George takes a moment to watch some of his nearby competitors.

There are a number of other Fishing Trawlers (some of which are changing direction and heading back to shore) and a large Cruise Liner making steady progress towards the horizon.

Just as George is considering a route that might take him closer to the horizon, a Power Boat whizzes by, leaving a spray of water as it goes.

As the Power Boat becomes a dot in the distance, George pulls off his sou'wester hat and replaces it with his old (but much more comfortable) baseball cap.

Rolling up his sleeves, he gets stuck into sorting the fish.

Later that day, when the crew have all gone home, George finally returns to his desk. After a day on deck, doing some 'real work', he feels exhilarated.

For the next few weeks, this is what he'll do. He can't rely on Liam or the others to sort out the catch anyway so it's better he gets back to it. Turning his baseball cap back to front, George suddenly has another idea.

His business may have a solid position and a decent regular customer base but his email box is full of enquiries so why not get back in the race – with a few more hours on the job every day, maybe he can get that increase in sales up to 50%!

Here's how George deals with three of those email enquiries:

> **Client 1** is an existing customer but, instead of their regular order, they want to know if George can up the quantity of fish by another 10,000 units. George replies saying of course he can fulfil the order. He'll get his whole team working on it and delivery by Monday is not a problem.

> **Client 2** is an old friend George knew from

his Power Boat days who asks George to help out with a job he's struggling with. It will only take a few weeks and, as well as a share of the catch, there's a pint with George's name on it at the end!

George replies saying of course he can help; he'll even come personally. After all, it will be a nice easy job (just like the old days). He's already looking forward to that pint!

Client 3 is a new prospect who asks if George wants to pitch for a trial order for halibut. If he is successful in the trial, George is guaranteed a much bigger regular order. George says of course he can help and arranges an appointment with the client.

The following day, George barks out the orders for his crew to haul in more nets than ever, then whizzes off on his mate's boat to help for the afternoon.

Later, George is about to spend his evening preparing the pitch for the new client when he remembers that they asked for halibut - a fish he knows nothing about.

In a panic, he realises the only way to get this order will be to bring in someone new – someone who has the knowledge and experience he doesn't have!

Commentary

George's Fishing Trawler has a strong hull which keeps the business and everyone in it safe from stormy conditions. He is effectively running a small business (Level 2) which has solid and stable foundations – a decent client base that is leading to increased sales, a marketable product, and a generally capable team on board.

However, the strength of the business relies too heavily on George's knowledge and skills.

He knows exactly what type of fish to look for and where to find them but also keeps this knowledge close to his chest.

In his mind, that's the only way to protect the business, ensuring they bring in the catch and make it back to dry land every day.

The good news is that, with his sou'wester hat on, George has started to take on some of the 'Manager' mindset. He's more forward thinking (looking at least six months ahead), has recruited a team to take on some key tasks and is investing some of his time in working on his business – looking at forecasts, targets and so on.

The problem is he doesn't always feel comfortable wearing that sou'wester and so ends up pulling the baseball cap back on, simultaneously falling back into the 'Supervisor' mindset.

He easily gets caught up in the minutia of the business again (sorting the fish). he's quick to go back to sale chasing and he's keep tight controls over everything.

He may have employed more people, but he really doesn't like the idea of putting his trust in them. So, he avoids passing on his knowledge and understanding to the team and panics at the idea of bringing in anyone that might know more than he does.

So, what should George do?

Well, everyone running a small or medium sized business will need to swap hats at some point. They may wear their Manager's hat to focus on long-term priorities but switch to a Supervisor's or Worker's hat to help out with some of the daily 'to do' list when necessary.

Transitioning up the Levels, however, requires the business owner to be aware of (and sometimes change) which hat they wear the most.

George's problem is he grabbed the baseball cap when he felt it was needed but became too comfortable wearing it again.

He's letting that Supervisor's mindset influence his long-term decisions, something that could throw his business out of balance at any moment. At least three out of the four drivers of his business currently need attention:

> **Time** – George still thinks of 'real work' as being all about fixing the boat, sorting the fish and cash counting. To grow his business,

this has to change.

George's 'real work' should now be about setting priorities for the business, keeping an eye on the vision, and developing plans that will take the business there (and he needs his sou'wester/Manager's hat firmly in place to do this).

Team – *George has a team in place but his ego is stopping him from developing them. He is unwilling to pass on his knowledge and understanding (and subsequently some of the control) to his team.*

This situation will see him constantly jumping in to fix things when others do them wrong. George must get over his ego! Instead of hiding things from his team, he needs to practice open communication, start sharing what his experience has taught him and offer training where it is needed. Wearing his Manager's hat, George should provide opportunities for his crew to step up (so that he can step up too).

George is also reluctant to employ someone

who has more experience or knowledge in a particular area than he has.

Somewhere out there is the person who could help him win the contract with that potentially lucrative new client but his ego and fear steps in.

He's afraid that this will challenge the perception people have of him as the one who does and knows everything! If George wants his business to survive the next period of growth, this is a challenge he must overcome.

Delivery – There is some value in the relationships George has built up with his clients and potential in the new enquiries he receives.

However, when he pulls the baseball cap back on, George goes back to chasing every available order with the classic 'No job is too big; no job is too small' outlook. The problem with this is two-fold:

1. George is failing to consider delivery in terms of total customer experience.

His 'can do' attitude may give a great first impression but taking on so many different orders will inevitably result in George having to let somebody down. It may even be a long-term client and that will make its mark on the profitability of the business.

2. George has lost the focus on where his boat is heading (the vision of the business). There may be lots of opportunities out there but what George needs to focus on is his vision and what type of client will help him get there the quickest.

Who, in fact, is his ideal client? If he's heading for the horizon, will helping his mate out for a few weeks really help him get there? If he can identify the ideal client for his business and focus on giving them the best possible experience of his business (exceeding their expectations rather than letting them down), you never know... he may just make it all the way to that Cruise Liner and reach for the Captain's hat too!

George heads to the shore
(but for how long?)

Some years later, we catch up with George and find he finally made it to that Cruise Liner, a ship that can safely navigate its way through large swells in the ocean and survive major storms relatively untouched.

There are now around 70 crew members and George wears his Captain's hat with ease.... well, some of the time!

For George, it took a lot of hard work to get where he is now.

He had to take control – real control – of his boat. That meant taking a step back to look at what would help his boat grow, then putting in the foundations that could achieve that.

George finally realised he had to invest – in systems, the crew and himself.

Now, he can finally rely on others to keep the boat afloat while he works on his long- term plan, setting priorities with targets for his team.

So, today, George has just spent a bit of time up on the Bridge but is happy to leave his First Mate and other senior crew members in charge for a while.

He's invested in his team so he's confident they know the priorities for the boat.

As he heads back to his cabin, George is already

thinking about where the ship is heading and how he can check if it's on course.

At his desk, he spends a good few hours poring over the latest market information and forecast. He spots an early warning sign that some stormy weather may lie ahead. It's slightly unpredictable but George knows it's best to be prepared. Immediately he radios up to the Bridge to explain the situation clearly and ask for their suggestions.

After consideration, the plan of action has been revised – the boat will still head for the same destination but the crew are now making some slight adjustments to the current course.

Happy that the changes will keep the boat secure, George spends some time with the passengers (his clients), all of whom are playing a key role in the profitability of the boat. They're being well looked after by members of the crew but

George knows it never does any harm for the Captain to put in an appearance.

He'll mingle for a while then invite one or two key clients to the Captain's table.

Because George's boat runs so well without him at the helm, he's able to spend much more time with his family.

His two children have grown up now so recently George and Kay managed to take a prolonged holiday – that tour of Europe they had been talking about for years!

Yes, George kept in touch while they were away but the First Mate handled things well and, in fact, exceeded their targets during this time. The long break has got George thinking.

He's still aiming to expand the company further (it's not quite at the end-goal yet) but isn't it time he took a bit more of a back seat and enjoyed a few more of those holidays on shore?

There's just one problem – who can he truly trust to take over?

Let's listen in to George and Kay talking this over

one evening:

Kay: Now, that's what I call a holiday! So nice to be away and not have the phone interrupting us all the time!

George: And the boat's still in one piece too!

Kay: See, I told you it would be. You've got some great people there, you know?

George: Definitely – they handled things brilliantly. The business just seems to be going from strength to strength and that's even without me being there!

Kay: So, why don't you just go ahead with the plan then – make that break a bit more permanent?

George: I know it's in the plan but...
(George pauses and walks across the room to where he's just spotted his old yellow sou'wester lying on top of a cabinet. He tries it on, putting his Captain's hat away in a drawer as he does).

George: I don't know. The Liner is at a really exciting stage of expansion – I probably need to be there to take things to the next level. Who knows the company as well as I do? Who's going to always make the right decisions and know what I would want or do? Who is going to work endlessly to make this expansion work?

Kay: George, take a breath! You're not the only one that knows what's good for the business any more. There's the First Mate for one thing. You said it yourself. He's brilliant at the job, got tons of experience and now he's proved he's capable of stepping up. Or there's the Operations Manager – he's been with you forever, hasn't he?

George: Tom?

Kay: Yes. Or, there's always Olivia – you know, your daughter – the one who has been living and breathing this business with you ever since she was five years old!

George: (*sighs*) I don't know, a holiday is one thing but this... it just feels weird. What am I going to do on dry land for so long anyway?

Ok, let's stop it there.

The conversation did, in fact, continue long into the night.

One-minute George would retrieve his Captain's hat and talk eagerly about passing over his responsibilities; the next he'd reach for the sou'wester and decide it wasn't possible – he'd just have to stay on board a while longer.

Commentary

George is clearly running a medium sized business at Level 3. The Cruise Liner has strong foundations and a vision which everyone on board is playing their part in achieving.

With his Captain's hat on, George displays the Manager/ Director's mindset, spending most of his time working on his business (rather than in it).

He's focused on where the boat is heading and sets the team priorities for how to get there. Importantly, he keeps a constant check for anything that might impact on his boat and is not afraid to change the plans when necessary. He maintains open communication with his team and because he has invested in them, he's comfortable in seeking their opinions and suggestions (most of the time).

To get to this Level, George had to make it through the hardest point of Transition - the change in mindset that allowed him to stop being the one to 'control' the day- to-day running of the business and become the one who 'controls' the overall direction of the business.

The problem he's facing now is very typical. The business is at a point where he could prepare it for sale or succession, meaning he could finally have the freedom to enjoy the lifestyle he has been working for.

George is seriously thinking about the idea of succession but finding it hard to face the fact that his boat could actually sail without him on board.

He doesn't really want to 'let go of the baby' and his indecision (and fears) are making his hat switching look like some kind of classic comedy scene.

So, what should George do?

In fact, George has already made the first step. He has invested in his boat and has the people and systems in place which ensure his business can survive without him. This point was proven when he took that long holiday and the boat not only kept sailing but thrived in his absence.

There are, however, some next steps which would help him overcome the urge to stay on board.

He needs to realise that succession is a process which requires planning. He can't just take the decision and hand over the hat one day.

Now, it looks like he has three possible successors and there's no denying it, it is going to be tricky for him to decide who is best. Should he reward the loyal crew member that has been at his side forever?

Should he choose his daughter – someone who surely shares his world view and will always make the right decision? Or should he go for the First Mate, the person who has the experience and knowledge to make their own decisions and has proven their capability in practice?

I actually think George already knows who is the best person to succeed in his Captain's role and that's why he has already given them opportunities to step up to the Bridge.

I could be wrong and it may be that he's planning for one of the others to take over. The important point to make is that, in managing succession, George needs to think about the impact it will have on his Cruise Liner as a whole and other members of the team.

His decision therefore, has to be made on fact rather than opinion, on merit rather than length of service or familial relationship alone.

If it turns out his daughter or the Operations Manager also has the skills, knowledge and experience required for the role then that's a different matter.

Whoever he chooses, the succession process requires George to practice open, honest communication so that everyone knows what to expect. This way, he can plan ahead and actually be in the right position to hand over his hat when everyone involved is ready.

The final point to make is that this is George's journey to a different lifestyle. Remember that being on shore doesn't mean doing nothing! He'll still have a role to play in directing the boat (or boats) as his business expands even further.

Watching the boats sail by

Years later, we see George sitting with Kay on the beach of a tropical island with his sun-hat on and reading the newspaper (he's checking out the latest share prices).

George now has a Fleet of Cruise Liners which employ more than 200 people between them. With perhaps the exception of a tsunami, the Fleet has such momentum that it can easily cope with pretty much any conditions at sea.

Once he'd got over the culture shock of handing over his Captain's hat, George took some time out to stop, reflect and review everything he'd done to get his first Cruise Liner, then multiplied it.

It was easy for him to get hold of a new ship, he knew what to look for in a new team and he had the experience required to give them the level of direction they needed.

In the end, the First Mate did succeed George as Captain of that first Liner.

It was a decision George didn't regret.

In fact, he's now on the verge of asking his former First Mate to oversee the entire Fleet (taking a Managing Director's role).

So, back on his tropical island, George is considering what the next decade may bring for the Fleet when he looks up and sees one of his ships as it drops anchor in the bay.

He's going to head out there a bit later, take a tour of the ship, meet some of the crew and... well, enjoy the hospitality of the Captain's table.

Coming up just behind the ship, George spots a Day Tripper full of happy holiday makers and an equally happy Skipper at the helm.

It's his son - Jack. Unlike his sister (and despite George's best efforts to get him involved), Jack never wanted to join the family business.

"What is that boy up to now?" George sighs as he and Kay wave out to sea. "One day" thinks Jack as he turns his gaze away from the Cruise Liner and waves back. "Now, where's that 'to do' list!"

Commentary

There's really not much more I could say to George. He's made it to Level 4, a larger medium sized business, by multiplying everything he's done so far.

George's sun hat now comes with an 'owner' mindset, something which continues to focus on the long-term but just on a bigger scale.

When the Cruise Liner became a Fleet, George put in a larger team of leaders and, in effect, his end-goal was reached!

His role now is to look even further into the future, setting priorities and offering guidance to those leaders when needed. His other role, of course, is to step back and enjoy the lifestyle and business he was aiming for all along!

If I was his business coach, at this point all I would have left to offer would be my huge congratulations... although I might just add one final question:

"*Shall I just keep a look-out for that son of yours?*"

"Get out of your comfort Zone"

Part 3 – The Moral of the Tale

Not all enterprises will grow through all the Levels in the way we've just watched George do so.

In fact, there are many successful businesses that sit comfortably at Levels 1 and 2 and have owners that are quite happy with what they've achieved.

There's nothing wrong with that!

If, however, you are the owner of an SME with an ambition to grow, think about George's story for a moment and ask yourself if you can identify with him at any point during his journey.

Perhaps you can picture yourself on the Power Boat and recognise the sacrifice to customer experience that often comes with chasing the sale and taking every order.

Or, maybe you can relate to the Fishing Boat's troubles - those times when you're supposed to be looking at annual targets but roll your sleeves up and get stuck into sorting the fish instead?

Maybe you don't identify with George's problems at all at the moment and think you're wearing the right hat for your business Level.

That's great but, if you're still planning to expand on what you have, you may have to make some changes you weren't anticipating.

Don't let that hat get too comfortable!

I hope that, through George's story, you will now have a better understanding of how a business can evolve as it makes it up the Levels and equally how the mindset of the owner must change too.

Being the owner of each of the different type of boats I've described comes with positives and negatives.

> As the owner of the Day Tripper, George was happy to be running everything on his own terms but the price to pay was the damaging cycle of feast and famine.

As the owner of the Power Boat, George felt the excitement that came with beating off the competition to the sale but the constant soaking left him with no time to maintain the boat, develop his team or have a life of his own!

As the owner of the Fishing Trawler, George had a team to help bring in the catch and weather the storm but his boat was still too dependent on his knowledge and skills Didn't his ego also quite like things that way?

As the owner of the Cruise Liner, George finally took control over the direction his boat was heading and had started to rely on his capable team.
But, the thorny issue of who could succeed him as Captain threatened to keep him on board longer than necessary.

Like any SME owner, George's role was often blurred - he was always going to wear different hats at different times (according to the needs of the business).

Now think about your own situation.

Regardless of how many links there are in your chain of command, as the owner of the business, you undoubtedly wear many of the different hats we saw George in (beanie, baseball cap, sou'wester and so on).

Every day, you probably find yourself switching hats without a second thought as different situations call for your attention!

The problems arise when you wear the wrong hat at the wrong time or for too long!

At times, we saw George pick up an old hat and become too comfortable wearing it. His focus retreated to the short- term, task-oriented lists - effectively taking his business back down a Level because things felt easier back then.

Other times he was so comfortable wearing his current hat and that it stopped him from moving the business up to the next Level.

On other occasions still, his hat switching became so rapid that it affected his ability to make longterm decisions.

From my years working with growing and developing businesses, I've seen all these situations in real-life... and many more. We've not even touched on the times when a business owner eagerly takes on the hat of a Level above their current position when their business just isn't ready for it.

Progressing up the Levels requires a process of Transition and if you're trying to grow your business, the hard work involved in this process just cannot be overlooked.

Ultimately, the key to navigating the Transition period (particularly from a Level 2 to Level 3 business) is about the proportion of your time you wear each hat and subsequently the proportion of time you spend working on or in your business.

When he wears the beanie or baseball cap for longer periods, George is spending more time on deck, 'doing' the business of the boat and less time managing the direction the boat is taking; when he wears the sou'wester or Captain's hat for longer, that allocation of his time starts to be reversed.

All of this is covered in much more detail in my other two Levels books, but taking George's story as inspiration, let me just summarise what you need to remember about getting through those difficult Transition periods and how to avoid getting stuck with the wrong hat:

Set out the stall – You need to prepare your business for a period of growth before it happens. That's done by looking at the foundations of the business and re-inforcing them so they can withstand a business that is larger than it is now.

Keep the balance – There are four drivers of your business (time, team, delivery and money) which, during a period of growth, have to remain balanced. This won't always be easy (especially during the Transition from Level 2 to 3).

Just look at how many issues George faced on his Fishing Boat – his time was being used ineffectively, his team were underdeveloped and his delivery was all over the place. If he hadn't been able to change his mindset, money would have been the next casualty!

Get out of the comfort zone – People often say they don't have time for the big stuff – there's too much to do, too much 'real work' to get on with (meaning they have to remain in the thick of things).

It's a classic case of the owner getting stuck in a business comfort zone with a mindset that is either lower than their actual business size or a mindset that cannot progress beyond their current business size.

They're wearing the wrong hat for too long – a sou'wester when they are already the Captain or a baseball cap when they should be reaching for the sou'wester.

This is a major issue for any business tackling

Transition. Making it up a Level requires the owner to get out of their comfort zone and start seeing their 'real work' as focusing on the long-term priorities for the business and what investment is needed for it to reach the vision.

(Note: Investment doesn't just mean money. It can also mean development of the team or investment of the owner's time.)

Face your fears – If you are the owner of a small but successful business, your ego will tell you all kinds of things that potentially stop it from developing any further.

Things are great as they are – the money's good, the lifestyle's good and people see you as the one who knows and can do everything – why change that?

OK, here's the truth – you are not the person who knows and can do everything (and cannot keep trying to be this person if you want to grow your business).

To make it through Transition, you will have

to pass on your own understanding of the business so that eventually you have a team you can rely on. Inevitably this also means employing people who know more about particular areas of the business than you do (either bringing in new people or developing existing staff). It's a scary thought but please face this fear and get over that ego!

Customers are key – It may be a bit of cliché but, in most cases, how you deal with customers will be a key component in managing the growth of your business. Think about what happened to George when he got too popular at the Day Tripping stage and had to turn people away.

Or what about the impact on delivery during his Power Boat days when he was busy chasing every order.

So, start thinking of customers in your business as more than just a sale and look at their whole experience with your company. Take time to identify who is your ideal client, then base your delivery around giving them the best experience possible – meeting and exceeding their expectations.

Stay focused but flexible - The business environment we operate in is in a constant state of flux and, to be successful, you have to be able to recognise this and evolve around it.

So, constantly seek up-to-date information (about the market, the trends, the forecast and so on).

This helps you to review and adapt your priorities, strategies and plans in line with whatever changes lie ahead (rather than reacting to them only when they fall upon you).

Have a clear vision and be firm in your decision to steer your business towards it. However, just as George did on the Cruise

Liner, don't be afraid to change course when needed. As long as you're still headed in the right direction, the plans for how you get there can remain fluid and flexible.

When the time comes, let go of the baby – You're the one who started this boat and you're the one who will take it to a position where it is ready to be passed on.

You don't have to go through sale or succession but, if this is in your plan, be prepared to let it go! Put time into planning the succession process and be sure to base your decisions over a successor on the facts.

Let me ask you once again – how much can you identify with George? What kind of boat are you running and what hat are you wearing most of the time?

The key to growing your company is so completely tied up with this last question.

Which hat you wear most of the time is

actually about where you position yourself in the company. How are you spending your time? How are you directing your team? How do you go about setting priorities for the business and everyone in it?

If your aim is to grow your business to a Cruise Liner or even a Fleet, now is the time to truly tackle that idea of 'real work', pick up the Captain's hat and try it out for size.

You never know, it may even suit you!

Further help

At Fluid Business, our team of proven business leaders and Levels Framework® experts can guide you through the process of Transition so you can build your business the way you want.

Using our industry leading toolbox of skills and coaching techniques, we'll give you the unbiased, external perspective you need to springboard your team and business to the next Level.

Find out more at: **fluidbusiness.co.uk**

About the Author

Ray Moore

After qualifying as a Management Accountant, Ray followed the traditional career path of working for large corporate businesses within various sectors including food manufacture, engineering and retail. He took an interesting, some might say risky, career choice to work for a successful serial entrepreneur who became his mentor and allowed Ray to understand his own natural business flair.

Over a ten-year collaboration, Ray built, bought and sold many businesses, the group grew to 340 employees and, as Financial Director, he was pivotal in finally selling it on to an FTSE 100 company.

This period saw Ray develop into a commercially minded businessman who had no desire to return to corporate life, so he quickly started his own business. Over the last 25 years, Ray has successfully set up, built and sold many more businesses. So, you could say he has been there, done that, got the t-shirt and a few scars along the way!

Fluid Business, Ray's current business, was developed from the desire to give business owners down to earth advice based on commercial reality rather than just theory. Bringing together the best business coached in the area, Fluid Business is now known for the unique and effective support it offers to business owners and their teams.

Ray's passion lies with family businesses especially in resolving conflict, managing family employees and succession planning. His personal experience of high growth and rapid change within his own organisations allows him to bring an independent and fresh perspective to these often-complex relationships.

Ray currently lives in Chelmsford, Essex with his wife, Jan. They are proud grandparents to seven grandchildren.

What Next?

If you're now inspired to find out exactly what
level your business is and where you should
focus your efforts to **achieve growth** then
T**he Levels Assessment®** can help
www.fluidbusiness.co.uk/levels_assessment

Currently a "**day tripper**" or "**power boat**" looking
to step up to the next level?
www.fluidbusinessacademy.com
will help you build the foundations needed for
sustainable growth

More publications from Ray Moore

The Levels: Can Your Business Step Up to the Growth Challenge?

The Levels focusses on challenges faced by business owners between the small to medium size transition-often a turbulent time for even the most accomplished entrepreneur!

A tried and tested model, author Ray Moore brings together his extensive knowledge, experience and challenges faced over his long and successful career in business ownership.

The Levels: Can YOU step up to the growth challenge?

In this book we see Ray turn his attention to the mindset changes business owners must embrace to achieve balanced growth in the same no nonsense, easy to understand style in this second book of the Levels series. Quite simply of all the things you are going to have to alter in your business, changing the way you think is going to be the most difficult. This is your route to taking control of the future - the future of your business and the lifestyle you really want to be living.